Searchlight BOOKS™

Animal
Superpowers

# Trap-Door
# Spiders

## and Other Amazing
## Predators

Rebecca E. Hirsch

Lerner Publications ◆ Minneapolis

Lerner Publications Company
A division of Lerner Publishing Group, Inc.
241 First Avenue North
Minneapolis, MN 55401 USA

For reading levels and more information, look up this title
at www.lernerbooks.com.


**Library of Congress Cataloging-in-Publication Data**

Names: Hirsch, Rebecca E., author.
Title: Trap-door spiders and other amazing predators / Rebecca E. Hirsch.
Description: Minneapolis, MN : Lerner Publications, [2017] | Series: Searchlight books.
    Animal Superpowers | Includes bibliographical references and index.
Identifiers: LCCN 2016016199 (print) | LCCN 2016021163 (ebook) | ISBN 9781512425482
    (lb : alk. paper) | ISBN 9781512431162 (pb : alk. paper) | ISBN 9781512428230 (eb pdf)
Subjects: LCSH: Predatory animals—Juvenile literature. | Animal defenses—Juvenile
    literature.
Classification: LCC QL758 .H568 2017 (print) | LCC QL758 (ebook) | DDC 591.5/3—dc23

LC record available at https://lccn.loc.gov/2016016199

Manufactured in the United States of America
1-41316-23260-5/27/2016

# Contents

# Chapter 1

# TRAP-DOOR SPIDERS

Predators are animals that catch and kill other animals. Predators catch prey in all sorts of ways. Sharp teeth and claws are only the beginning. Some predators disguise themselves and lure their prey in close. Some poison their prey or knock it out with a powerful punch. The trap-door spider builds a special trap to catch its next meal.

**Trap-door spiders are predators. How do they catch their prey?**

Trap-door spiders don't catch their prey in webs the way some spiders do. Instead, they build an underground tunnel with a hidden trapdoor. The door is camouflaged with sticks, pebbles, or bits of plants. The spider hides behind the door and waits. It holds the door closed with its mouthparts. The spider waits for an insect or other prey to come near.

This trap-door spider sits inside its tunnel.

A beetle crawls near the spider's burrow. It doesn't see the hidden door. When the beetle reaches the door, its movement creates vibrations. The waiting spider cannot see or smell the beetle. But it can feel the vibrations.

Without warning, the door bursts open. The spider lunges out. It grabs the beetle and drags it back down into the tunnel. The door closes automatically behind it.

It takes less than a second for a trap-door spider to capture its prey.

## Building the Trap

Different kinds of trap-door spiders live across the southern and southwestern United States. All of them build secret chambers to catch prey. Each spider chooses a bank or hillside near an animal trail where prey might pass.

**A trap-door spider may hunt beetles, ants, other spiders, and small lizards.**

To build its hidden tunnel, the trap-door spider digs using its mouthparts. It rolls the dirt into pellets and throws them from the hole. Next, the spider strengthens the tunnel walls with a mixture of dirt and saliva. Then it adds a layer of spider silk to make the tunnel even stronger.

A trap-door spider digs with its mouthparts and throws dirt from the hole with its hind legs.

Next, the trap-door spider builds a hidden door out of silk and soil. It adds a silk hinge so the door will open and close easily. The spider camouflages the door with twigs and bits of dead plants. This makes the door hard to spot. Some trap-door spiders build a simple tunnel with a single door. Some build a long tunnel with more than one door.

THE SILK TRAPDOOR WILL OPEN AND
CLOSE QUICKLY FOR THE SPIDER.

Trap-door spiders also hide inside their tunnels from other predators. Female spiders use the tunnel as a nursery for their young. They lay their eggs in the burrow. The young remain with their mother in the burrow. They leave when they are ready to hunt on their own.

**This female trap-door spider raises her young inside her burrow.**

# Compare It!

Saltwater crocodiles also hide to catch their prey. These large reptiles hunt in the Pacific Ocean near Australia. They swim with their bodies underwater. Only their eyes, ears, and nose are above the water. When prey comes to the water's edge, a crocodile quietly swims closer. Then it lunges out of the water, snaps its heavy jaws, and drags its catch into the water.

Saltwater crocodiles eat birds, sea turtles, monkeys, horses, cows, and water buffalo. They even eat sharks!

# Chapter 2

# DEEP-SEA ANGLERFISH

A deep-sea anglerfish swims through black water. This unusual creature has a huge head and a large mouth lined with sharp teeth. Something like a fishing rod grows out of its head. The tip of the rod is a glowing, pulsing blob of light.

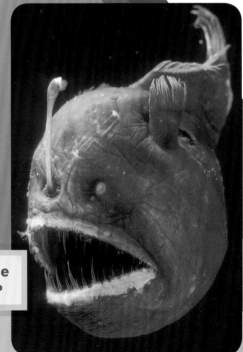

A deep-sea anglerfish lives in the dark. How does it find its way?

The anglerfish lives in one of the most extreme places on Earth. It lives up to 1 mile (1.6 kilometers) deep in the ocean. At this depth, the water is freezing cold and pitch black. There is no sunlight.

Because it is so dark, lots of animals this deep in the ocean provide their own light. The anglerfish's fishing rod is really a piece of fin that sticks out above its mouth. The glowing tip is a piece of flesh filled with millions of glowing bacteria. Along with providing light, the glowing rod also lures an anglerfish's prey.

Fish, squid, and shrimp are drawn to an anglerfish's light.

## Deep-Sea Fishing

As the anglerfish swims, it dangles the fishing rod over its wide-open mouth. It wiggles the glowing blob back and forth. A small fish swims closer. It is drawn to the light. It does not notice the open jaws of the anglerfish. The fish touches the rod. The anglerfish lunges, and its jaws snap shut. It has caught its dinner.

**The jaws of the anglerfish close automatically when a fish touches the rod.**

# Compare It!

An alligator snapping turtle also lures its dinner with part of its body.  The alligator snapping turtle's lure is a bright pink piece of flesh in its gray mouth.  The flesh looks like a worm.  The turtle waits on the bottom of the water with its mouth open wide.  It wiggles the pink flesh.  When curious frogs or fish come closer to investigate, the turtle snaps its jaws closed.

**This alligator snapping turtle waits for its prey to come near.**

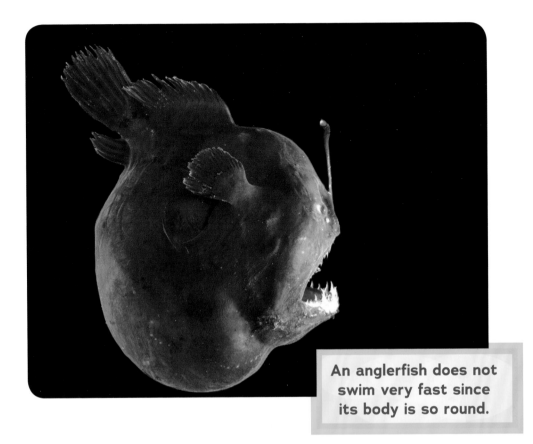

An anglerfish does not swim very fast since its body is so round.

More than two hundred kinds of anglerfish swim in the sea. Anglerfish of every kind have a rod to catch fish. They have big mouths and flexible bodies. Some anglerfish can swallow prey up to twice their own size. Their stomachs expand to hold their catch.

Only female anglerfish have a "fishing rod" growing out of their heads. Male anglerfish are tiny. They don't find food by fishing. Instead, a male uses his sense of smell to find a female. When he finds a female, he hooks onto her body with his teeth. He releases a substance that fuses his mouth to her body. He lives as a parasite, sucking nutrients from her body.

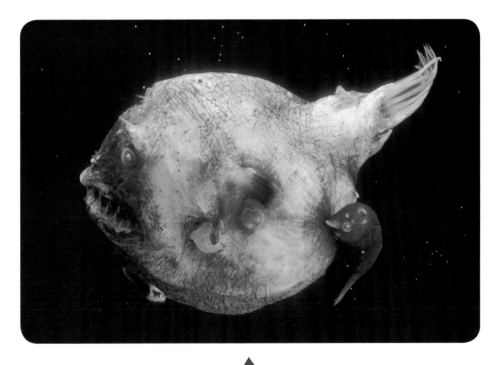

A TINY MALE ANGLERFISH LIVES AS A PARASITE ON A FEMALE ANGLERFISH.

# Chapter 3

# MANTIS SHRIMP

Two eyes peek out of a crack in a coral reef. It is a peacock mantis shrimp. Its 6-inch (15-centimeter) body is a rainbow of colors. Two club-like arms are folded against its body. Its big eyes watch for prey. Each eye turns independently—up, down, left, and right.

The peacock mantis shrimp is a very colorful creature. Where does it live?

A reef crab wanders close to the mantis shrimp's burrow. The shrimp crawls out. It advances on the crab. *Bang!* In a split second, the shrimp has cracked the thick shell of the crab. A few more punches and the crab's shell opens to reveal its soft body. The shrimp pulls its dinner back into its burrow.

A REEF CRAB CAN BE PREY FOR THE PEACOCK MANTIS SHRIMP.

## Knockout Punch

The mantis shrimp is one of the fastest punchers on the planet. The mantis shrimp stores energy in its club-like claws. Then it releases each club in a springlike motion and delivers a knockout punch to its prey. With the help of a high-speed video camera, scientists clocked the punch at speeds of 50 miles (80 km) per hour, or 76 feet (23 meters) per second. That gives the punch the force of a .22 caliber bullet!

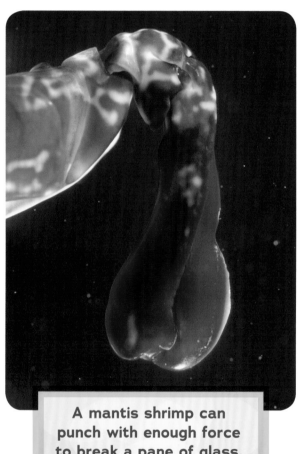

**A mantis shrimp can punch with enough force to break a pane of glass.**

# Compare It!

The peregrine falcon is another predator that uses speed to catch its dinner. The falcons are famous for fast flying. A peregrine falcon can pursue prey, such as pigeons and doves, at 69 miles (112 km) per hour. It reaches its top speeds when diving on prey from above. One falcon was clocked diving at 242 miles (389 km) per hour. That's as fast as a speeding race car!

**This peregrine falcon searches for its prey.**

There are two main kinds of mantis shrimp, based on the shape of their claws: smashers and spearers. Spearers have spear-like forelimbs. When soft-bodied prey comes near, a spearer can flick out its pointy limb and stab a fish before the fish even knows it is there.

**Mantis shrimp only look like shrimp. They are actually a kind of animal called a stomatopod.**

Smashers, such as the peacock mantis shrimp, have club-like claws. They can club with enough power to crack open hard-shelled prey like crabs, clams, and snails. The force of the punch creates a wall of bubbles. As the bubbles hit the target, they give off a burst of heat, a flash of light, and a bang. The extra blow from the bubbles helps crack open the hard shell. That is one powerful punch!

The mantis shrimp smashes open its prey and feeds on its soft body.

# Chapter 4

# KOMODO DRAGONS

A Komodo dragon hides in tall grass beside an animal trail. The dragon remains still, waiting for its next meal to walk by. An animal approaches along the trail. The dragon's muscles tense. When the animal is near, the dragon leaps out. It attacks the animal's feet and knocks the surprised animal to the ground.

A Komodo dragon has a strong, powerful neck. How does it use its neck to help it hunt?

The Komodo dragon grabs the animal with its sharp claws. It bites down with its sharp teeth. Then it uses its strong neck to pull back its head and open a gaping wound on the animal.

A KOMODO DRAGON CAN GROW LONGER THAN 10 FEET (3 M).

Komodo dragons are the largest lizards in the world. They use stealth and strength to catch their prey. Young dragons catch rodents and other small prey. As they grow bigger, they catch larger prey. Full-grown Komodo dragons will eat deer, goats, pigs, water buffalo, and sometimes other Komodo dragons. All Komodo dragons will scavenge carcasses killed by other animals.

A Komodo dragon's teeth are curved and notched like shark teeth.

## Deadly Drool

The dragon's poisonous bite makes the attack even deadlier. Hidden in the dragon's lower jaw are glands filled with venom. When the dragon bites, venom drips into the wound. If the prey escapes, the venom prevents the prey's blood from clotting (becoming a solid). As the wounded animal flees, it loses blood and grows weaker. The animal may pass out.

Meanwhile, the Komodo dragon follows. It flicks its tongue in and out. It is sampling scent molecules in the air to follow the dying animal. It can smell the dead or dying animal up to 2.5 miles (4 km) away.

**This Komodo dragon is smelling the air with its tongue.**

Once the dragon tracks down its prey, it eats. More Komodo dragons may join the feast, attracted by the smell. They are big eaters. Their stomachs expand, allowing Komodo dragons to eat up to 80 percent of their own body weight in a single meal.

KOMODO DRAGONS EAT ALMOST EVERY PART OF THEIR PREY, INCLUDING BONES AND HOOVES.

# Compare It!

The Amazonian giant centipede also uses power, stealth, and venom. These 1-foot-long (30 cm) insects live on the forest floor. They look for tarantulas, toads, birds, lizards, and rodents to eat. They sometimes dangle from cave ceilings and snatch bats out of the air. The centipede anchors itself to the cave ceiling with at least five pairs of back legs. It catches bats with its front pairs of legs. Then it paralyzes the bat using venom from its sharp claws.

A giant centipede can catch prey up to twice its weight.

# Chapter 5

# KILLER WHALES

Three orcas swim around a floating chunk of ice in the Antarctic Ocean. On the ice, a seal is resting. The orcas gather together under the water. With a burst of speed, they swim toward the ice. Their bodies create a big wave. Just before reaching the ice, the orcas dive. The wave of water crashes over the ice. The wave sweeps the seal into the water.

Orcas, also called killer whales, live in groups. What are their groups called?

Orcas are fierce predators of the seas. The largest of all dolphins, orcas live in groups called pods. Orcas use brain power and teamwork when they hunt. They can catch many types of marine animals. They eat sharks, whales, seals, sea lions, penguins, squid, and octopuses.

**Orcas can hunt and kill many different animals, including penguins.**

Orcas hunt in different ways, depending on their prey. When they hunt dangerous animals, like sharks, they keep out of harm's way. An orca can drive a shark to the surface without touching it. The orca swims upward, creating a current with its tail. This carries the shark to the surface. Then the orca turns and smacks the shark on the head with its tail. Finally, it flips the shark over, which instantly paralyzes the shark. Then the shark is safe for the killer whale to eat.

**The body shape of an orca is efficient for moving through water.**

Orcas can even hunt seals and sea lions on land. To catch a seal or sea lion on a beach, an orca charges the shore and launches itself onto the beach. It snatches the prey. Then it flaps and hops to slide its body back into the water.

ORCAS BEACH THEMSELVES TO CATCH PREY ON LAND.

## Cooperation Is Key

Orcas often cooperate to hunt prey. When catching herring, a small fish that lives in schools, orcas work together. The herring are too fast for orcas to catch directly. So they use their bodies to herd the herring into a tight ball. A slap of the tail stuns fish on the edge of the ball. Some in the pod eat the stunned fish while the others keep herding the fish.

**Orcas herd herring into a tight ball to make them easier to eat.**

# Compare It!

As with killer whales, spotted hyenas cooperate to catch a wide variety of prey. Hyenas switch tactics depending on the size of their group. The bigger the pack of hyenas, the larger its prey. Large packs chase down zebras and young rhinos. Smaller packs hunt gazelles and impalas. A lone hyena may catch rabbits and porcupines. Hyenas can chase their prey over long distances at up to 37 miles (60 km) per hour. While they run, they might bite at their prey's legs until the animal turns to face them. Then the hyenas work together to take down their prey.

**Hyenas often target animals that look weak.**

## Fearsome Predators

From killer whales to mantis shrimp, predators come in all shapes and sizes, but all hunt to survive. They use all sorts of wild and amazing superpowers to pursue prey. Sharp teeth and claws are only the beginning. With poison, clever traps, glowing lures, or deadly teamwork, these superpowered predators are as fearsome as they come.

WHAT OTHER AMAZING
PREDATORS CAN YOU THINK OF?

# Extinct Animal Superpowers

- An ancient relative of the saltwater crocodile called *Sarcosuchus* stretched as long as a school bus and weighed as much as 10 tons (9 metric tons). It hunted the same way saltwater crocodiles do, by staying hidden under the water.

- *Tyrannosaurus rex*, one of the largest dinosaur predators ever, may have hunted in packs. Some scientists think that could explain how *T. rex* was able to kill dinosaurs larger than itself.

- *Megalania* was the largest lizard ever known to walk on land. Like the Komodo dragon, it probably used venom to kill its prey.

# Glossary

**bacteria:** tiny, single-celled organisms that live in soil, water, and the bodies of plants and animals

**burrow:** a hole in the ground made by an animal

**camouflage:** to hide or disguise something by covering it up or changing the way it looks

**cooperate:** to act together with others to get something done

**paralyze:** to make unable to move

**parasite:** a living thing that lives in or on another living thing

**predator:** an animal that kills and eats other animals

**prey:** an animal that is hunted and killed for food

**scavenge:** to search for food to eat

**venom:** poison produced by some animals and passed to a victim usually by biting or stinging. A Komodo dragon uses venom.

LERNER
SOURCE

Expand learning beyond the printed book. Download free, complementary educational resources for this book from our website, www.lernerresource.com.

# Learn More about Predators

## Books

Johnson, Rebecca L. *When Lunch Fights Back: Wickedly Clever Animal Defenses*. Minneapolis: Millbrook Press, 2015. Learn more about the mantis shrimp and other animals that are amazingly good at self-defense.

Marsh, Laura F. *Weird Sea Creatures*. Washington, DC: National Geographic, 2012. Learn more about the deep-sea anglerfish and other strange creatures that live in the sea.

Pallotta, Jerry. *Killer Whale vs. Great White Shark*. New York: Scholastic, 2016. In this book, you can find out what would happen in a matchup of two of the ocean's most fearsome predators.

## Websites

*National Geographic*—World's Deadliest: Shrimp Packs a Punch
http://video.nationalgeographic.com/video/worlds-deadliest/deadliest-mantis-shrimp?source=relatedvideo
Watch this video to see the mantis shrimp let loose its superpowered punch.

*National Geographic Kids*—Orca
http://kids.nationalgeographic.com/animals/orca/#orca-jumping.jpg
Learn more about one of the ocean's most famous predators, including how orcas hunt and cooperate.

Wildscreen ARKive
http://www.arkive.org
This site features photos, video, and audio clips of many amazing animal predators.

# Index

# Photo Acknowledgments

The images in this book are used with the permission of: © Barry Mansell/SuperStock, p. 4; © B. G. Thomson/Science Source, p. 5; © James H. Robinson/Science Source, p. 6; Ken Griffiths/NHPA/Photoshot/Newscom, p. 7; © Dr. Paul Zahl/Science Source, p. 8; © Hans Christoph Kappel/Minden Pictures, p. 9; © Francesco Tomasinelli/Science Source, p. 10; © 2630ben/iStock/Thinkstock, p. 11; © Norbert Wu/Minden Pictures, pp. 12, 13, 17, 31; © David Shale/Minden Pictures, pp. 14, 16; © Daniel Heuclin/Minden Pictures, p. 15; © Andaman/Shutterstock.com, p. 18; © iStockphoto.com/Tammy616, p. 19; S. Zankl/picture alliance/blickwinkel/S/Newscom, p. 20; © iStockphoto.com/SteveOehlenschlager, p. 21; © WhitcombeRD/iStock/Thinkstock, p. 22; © Daniela Dirscherl/WaterFrame/Getty Images, p. 23; © Chien Lee/Minden Pictures, p. 24; © Sergey Uryadnikov/Shutterstock.com, pp. 25, 28; © Sylvain Cordier/Minden Pictures, p. 26; © iStockphoto.com/bdbecker, p. 27; © Robert Clay/Alamy, p. 29; © Doug Allan/Minden Pictures, p. 30; © Flip Nicklin/Minden Pictures, p. 32; © Gabriel Rojo/Minden Pictures, p. 33; © Rich Carey/Shutterstock.com, p. 34; © Denis-Huot/Minden Pictures, p. 35; © iStockphoto.com/jez_bennett, p. 36; © De Agostini Picture Library/Universal Images Group North America LLC/Alamy, p. 37.

Front cover: © zstock/Shutterstock.com.

Main body text set in Adrianna Regular 14/20.
Typeface provided by Chank.